D1065339

RHINOS

Published by Creative Education, Inc., 123 South Broad Street, Mankato, Minnesota
56001

Printed by permission of Wildlife Education, Ltd.

ISBN 0-88682-333-1

RHINOS

Created and Written by
John Bonnett Wexo

Zoological Consultant
Charles R. Schroeder, D.V.M.
Director Emeritus
San Diego Zoo &
San Diego Wild Animal Park

Scientific Consultants
Michael Dee
Senior Animal Keeper
Los Angeles Zoo

Carmi Penny
Curator
San Diego Zoo

Ian Player, D.M.S.
Executive Director
Wilderness Leadership School
Durban, South Africa

Creative Education

Art Credits

Pages Eight and Nine: Barbara Hoopes; **Background Map and Top:** Walter Stuart; **Pages Ten and Eleven:** Michael Woods; **Page Ten: Middle and Bottom Left,** Walter Stuart; **Page Eleven: Top,** Walter Stuart; **Pages Twelve and Thirteen:** Michael Woods; **Page Twelve: Middle Left,** Walter Stuart; **Page Thirteen: Top,** Walter Stuart; **Pages Fourteen and Fifteen:** Michael Woods; **Page Fourteen: Bottom Left,** WalterStuart; **Page Fifteen: Top,** Walter Stuart; **Pages Sixteen and Seventeen:** Michael Woods; **Page Sixteen: Bottom Left,** Walter Stuart; **Page Eighteen: Top Right,** Michael Woods; **Bootom Left,** Walter Stuart; **Page Nineteen:** Michael Woods.

Photographic Credits

Front Cover; Mohamed Amin *(Bruce Coleman, Inc.):* **Pages Six and Seven:** Norman Owen Tomalin *(Bruce Coleman, Inc.)*: **Page Ten:** Sven-Olof Lindblad *(Photo Researchers);* **Page Fourteen: Top,** A.J.S. Weaving *(Ardea London);* **Bottom,** Jane Burton *(Bruce Coleman, Ltd.);* **Page Fifteen:** M. Philip Kahl, Jr. *(Photo Researchers);* **Page Seventeen: Top,** Rod Allin *(Tom Stack & Associates);* **Middle,** Nancy Adams *(Tom Stack & Associates);* **Bottom,** Su Gooders *(Ardea London);* **Page Eighteen: Middle Left,** Alain Compost *(Bruce Coleman, Ltd.);* **Middle Right,** Bettman Archive; **Bottom,** Francois Gohier *(Photo Researchers);* **Page Nineteen:** Nadine Orabona *(Tom Stack & Associates);* **Pages Twenty and Twenty-one:** McDougal Tiger Tops *(Ardea London);* **Page Twenty-two and Twenty-three:** Clem Haagner *(Bruce Coleman, Inc.).*

Our Thanks To: Jean Vertut; Deanna Cross and Mary de G. White *(Metropolitan Museum of Art);* Dr. Rama Rao *(Washington State University);* Indian Tourist Office, Los Angeles; Dr. Jim Dolan *(General Curator, San Diego Zoo);* Michaele Robinson and Janet Lombard *(San Diego Zoo Library);* and Lynnette Wexo.

Creative Education would like to thank Wildlife Education, Ltd., for granting them the rights to print and distribute this hardbound edition.

Contents

Rhinos are powerful and impressive animals. When you look at a rhino, you just can't help feeling a great deal of respect for its sheer size and strength.

There are five living types (or species) of rhinos: the White, Black, Indian, Javan and Sumatran. The largest of all is probably the White rhino. These magnificent creatures can grow larger than any other land mammals, except elephants. A fully grown White rhino may stand 6 feet tall at the shoulder (183 centimeters), and it can weigh almost *8 thousand pounds* (3600 kilograms). That means it can weigh as much as *50 average-size men*.

Indian rhinos can be even taller than White rhinos. They may grow to a height of 6 feet 6 inches (198 centimeters). But they don't weigh as much as White rhinos. The heaviest Indian rhino on record weighed "only" 6900 pounds (3130 kilograms) — so the Indian rhinoceros has to be called the *second* largest rhino species.

No matter what the size of a rhinoceros is, it has certain things in common with all other rhinos. Every rhino has a large head, a short neck, a broad chest, and very thick legs. All rhinos are also vegetarians. They eat only plants and never touch meat.

Can you guess what the name rhinoceros means? Does it describe the feet of rhinos, their tails, or their horns? You'll probably answer "horns," because rhinos are most famous for their horns — and you'll be right. The word *rhinoceros* is made up of two ancient Greek words that mean "nose" (*rhino*) and "horn" (*ceros*). And this is only fitting, since rhinos are the only animals on earth that have horns on their noses. All other animals with horns have them on top of their heads.

Unfortunately, the wonderful horns that make rhinos so unique are also dangerous for them. To get the horns, some people in Africa and Asia have been killing rhinos in large numbers. And this has pushed all five species of rhinos very close to the brink of extinction. Javan and Sumatran rhinos are among the most endangered animals on earth.

The five types of rhinos have much smaller ranges than they had in the past—and the number of rhinos living in the ranges is much smaller. Black rhinos were once found throughout eastern and southern Africa. But they now live in several dozen small areas. The ranges of White, Indian, Javan and Sumatran rhinos are so tiny that you may have trouble finding them on the map.

It's easy to tell one type of rhino from another. Just look at the shapes of their heads and horns. Notice that three species have two horns, while the others have only one horn. Males and females have the same number of horns, except Javan rhinos. Javan females don't have any horns at all.

WHITE RHINO

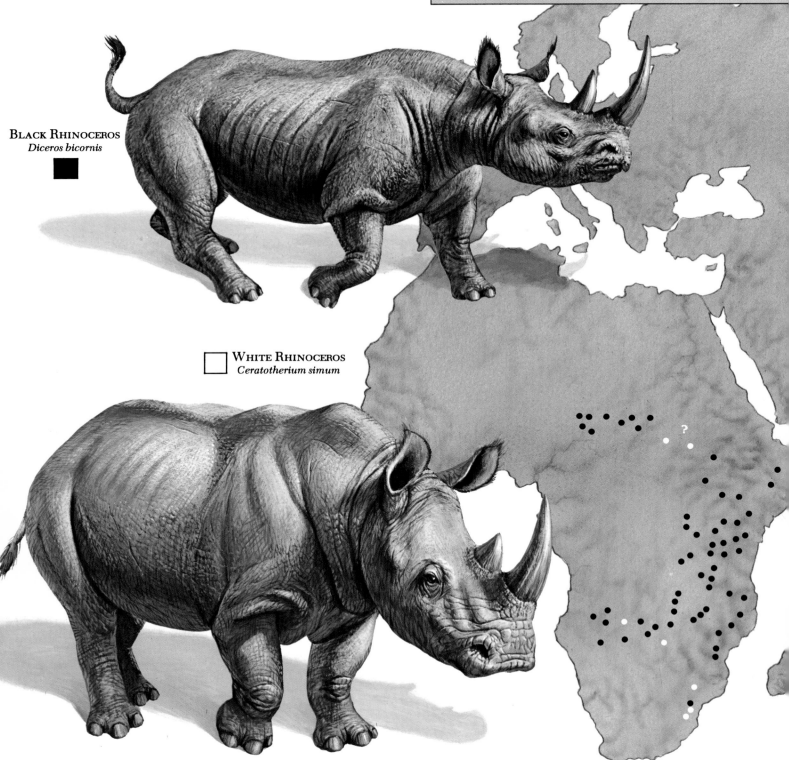

BLACK RHINOCEROS
Diceros bicornis

WHITE RHINOCEROS
Ceratotherium simum

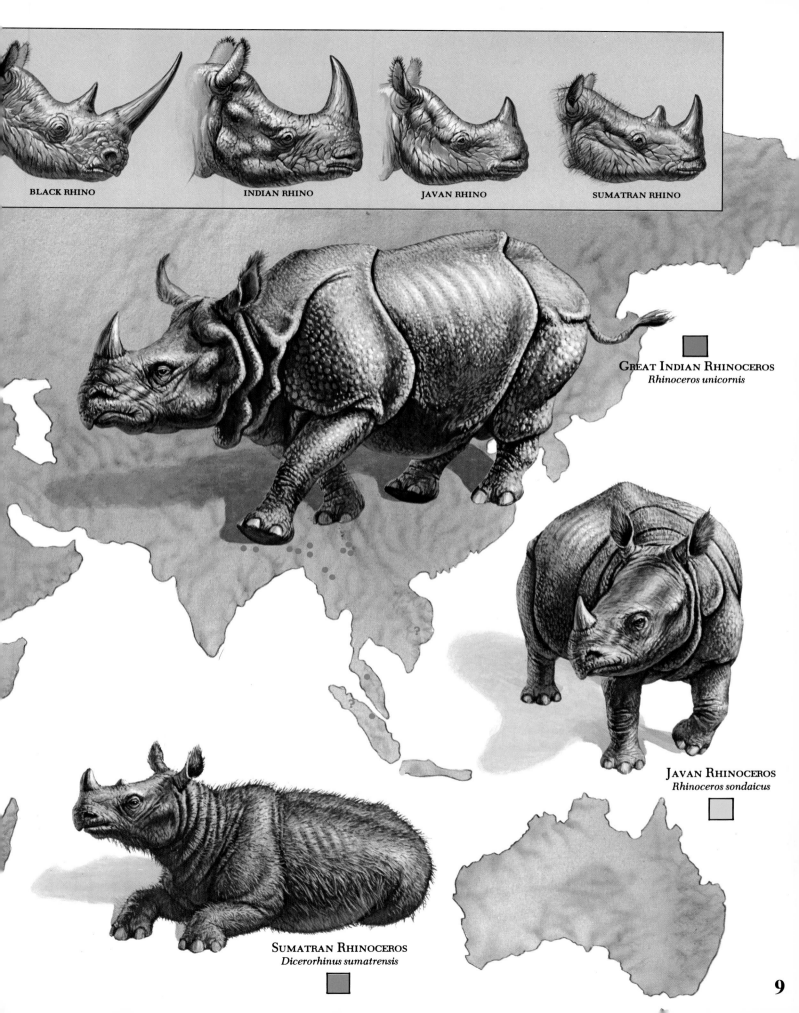

BLACK RHINO   INDIAN RHINO   JAVAN RHINO   SUMATRAN RHINO

GREAT INDIAN RHINOCEROS
Rhinoceros unicornis

JAVAN RHINOCEROS
Rhinoceros sondaicus

SUMATRAN RHINOCEROS
Dicerorhinus sumatrensis

9

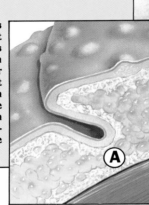

Rhinos are built for power. A

great deal of their enormous weight is solid muscle. There are very strong muscles to drive the legs and exceptionally large muscles on the back to move the large head. (Can you find these muscles?)

Beneath the muscles, a rhino has thick bones. The leg bones are particularly thick because they must carry the animal's weight. As you might expect, the skull of a rhino is huge and heavily built. And it has lots of big teeth for crushing its food.

People often think of rhinos as "living tanks" that have armor-plated skin. Indian and Javan Rhinos look especially like tanks. Their skin seems to be divided into plates, and the bumps on the skin look like rivets.

The skin of rhinos is very thick, but not nearly as strong as armor plate. It can be scratched rather easily—and most rhinos have scars on their hides to prove it. The "joints" in the surface are really just folds in the skin Ⓐ.

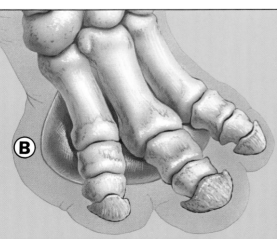

Inside their hooves, rhinos have three toes. A soft pad under the toes Ⓑ cushions the foot and helps to carry the tremendous weight of the animal.

It might surprise you to learn that horses and rhinos are very closely related to each other. Like horses, rhinos walk and run on their toes —and they can run very fast. Even the biggest rhinos may reach a speed of 35 miles per hour (56 kilometers). This is as fast as most horses can run, although a horse can keep running at this speed much longer than a rhino can.

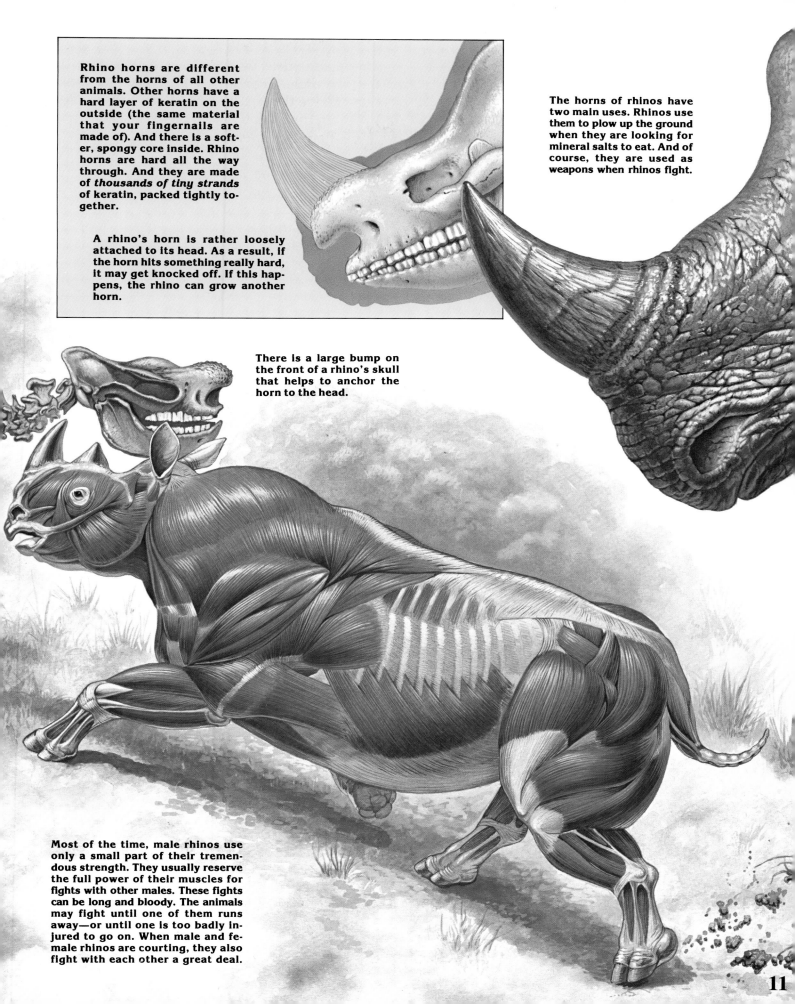

Rhino horns are different from the horns of all other animals. Other horns have a hard layer of keratin on the outside (the same material that your fingernails are made of). And there is a softer, spongy core inside. Rhino horns are hard all the way through. And they are made of *thousands of tiny strands* of keratin, packed tightly together.

A rhino's horn is rather loosely attached to its head. As a result, if the horn hits something really hard, it may get knocked off. If this happens, the rhino can grow another horn.

The horns of rhinos have two main uses. Rhinos use them to plow up the ground when they are looking for mineral salts to eat. And of course, they are used as weapons when rhinos fight.

There is a large bump on the front of a rhino's skull that helps to anchor the horn to the head.

Most of the time, male rhinos use only a small part of their tremendous strength. They usually reserve the full power of their muscles for fights with other males. These fights can be long and bloody. The animals may fight until one of them runs away—or until one is too badly injured to go on. When male and female rhinos are courting, they also fight with each other a great deal.

In the past, there were many more kinds of rhinos than there are today. Instead of just five species, there were hundreds of species. As you can see, some of the ancient rhinos looked like today's rhinos, and some of them did not.

The first rhinos lived about 60 million years ago. They were very small and looked like the ancestors of horses. They did not have horns, and many rhinos that came after them did not have horns, either. Some ancient rhinos had much longer legs than today's rhinos, and some had much shorter legs. Can you find some other differences between ancient and modern rhinos?

GIANT GIRAFFE-RHINOCEROS
Indricotherium

The largest land mammal that ever lived was part of the rhino family. It was about 18 feet tall at the shoulder (5.5 meters) and 28 feet long (8.5 meters) —roughly the size of two school buses! This giant is called Indricotherium (in-DRIK-o-theer-ee-um).

MARSH RHINOCEROS
Metamynodon

WOOLY RHINOCEROS
Coelodonta

SHORT-LEGGED RHINOCEROS
Teleoceras

The first rhinos lived in North America. Over the course of time, some types of ancient rhinos migrated to Asia. All living rhinos are descended from these animals. The last rhinos in North America became extinct about 5 million years ago.

At one time or another, ancient rhinos lived on many of the world's continents (the green areas on the map). As far as we know, there have never been rhinos in South America, Australia, or Antarctica.

BIG HORN RHINOCEROS
Elasmotherium

SLENDER RHINOCEROS
Juxia

ETRUSCAN RHINOCEROS
Dicerorhinus

RUNNING RHINOCEROS
Hyracodon

TWIN-HORNED RHINOCEROS
Diceratherium

LONG-NOSED RHINOCEROS
Meninatherium

PRIMITIVE RHINOCEROS
Hyrachyus

Black rhinos are *browsers*. They prefer to eat bushes and trees instead of grass. To do this, a Black rhino has a prehensile (pre-HEN-sill) lip that works like a large finger. The lip grabs twigs and shoves them into the mouth, so the teeth can bite them off. When their favorite foods are hard to find, Black rhinos may eat grass—and the "finger" is used to rip up clumps of grass (as shown at left).

Black rhinos live on the plains of Africa, where they do the same kinds of things that all rhinos do. They spend the hottest hours of every day sleeping, and most of the remaining time eating huge quantities of food.

These animals are famous for their bad tempers. Black rhinos don't seem to like anything or anybody — including other Black rhinos. Sometimes, 2 or 3 of them may live together. But most of the time each Black rhino lives by itself, and seems to prefer it that way.

Black rhinos are also famous for their terrible eyesight. They may be the most nearsighted animals in Africa. At a distance of only 15 feet (4.6 meters), they don't seem able to tell a man from a tree.

Some scientists believe that rhinos have such poor eyesight because their ancestors lived in dense forests. In such places, the thick cover of plants prevents animals from seeing very far in any direction—so good eyesight isn't really necessary.

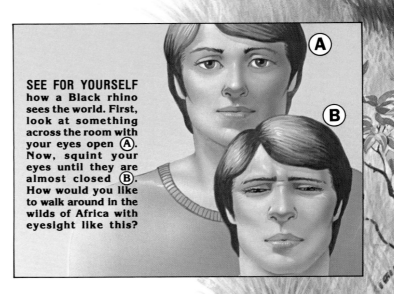

SEE FOR YOURSELF how a Black rhino sees the world. First, look at something across the room with your eyes open Ⓐ. Now, squint your eyes until they are almost closed Ⓑ. How would you like to walk around in the wilds of Africa with eyesight like this?

The common names of African rhinos are not really accurate. Black rhinos are not black. And White rhinos are not white. The skin on both species is actually a *dull gray*. However, since rhinos like to take mud baths and dust baths, they often take on the color of the ground where they live. For this reason, they may look red, or brown, or purple—or a lot of other colors.

You may think that rhinos don't look very tender. But rhino mothers are among the best in the animal world. They may keep their young with them for years. And during that time, they teach the young everything they will need to know to survive on their own. Usually, the young don't leave their mothers until the mothers give birth to new babies. By that time, the young rhinos may be almost as big as their mothers.

Hold on to your hat when a rhino starts chasing after you! Rhinos can charge with such force that they can easily over-turn a car or small truck.

The bad temper of a rhino and its bad eyesight may be connected. Until a rhino is almost on top of something, it can't really tell if that something is friendly or not. So rhinos may charge every-thing just to be on the safe side. Many times, rhinos have been seen charging at trees and large rocks, trying to scare them away!

15

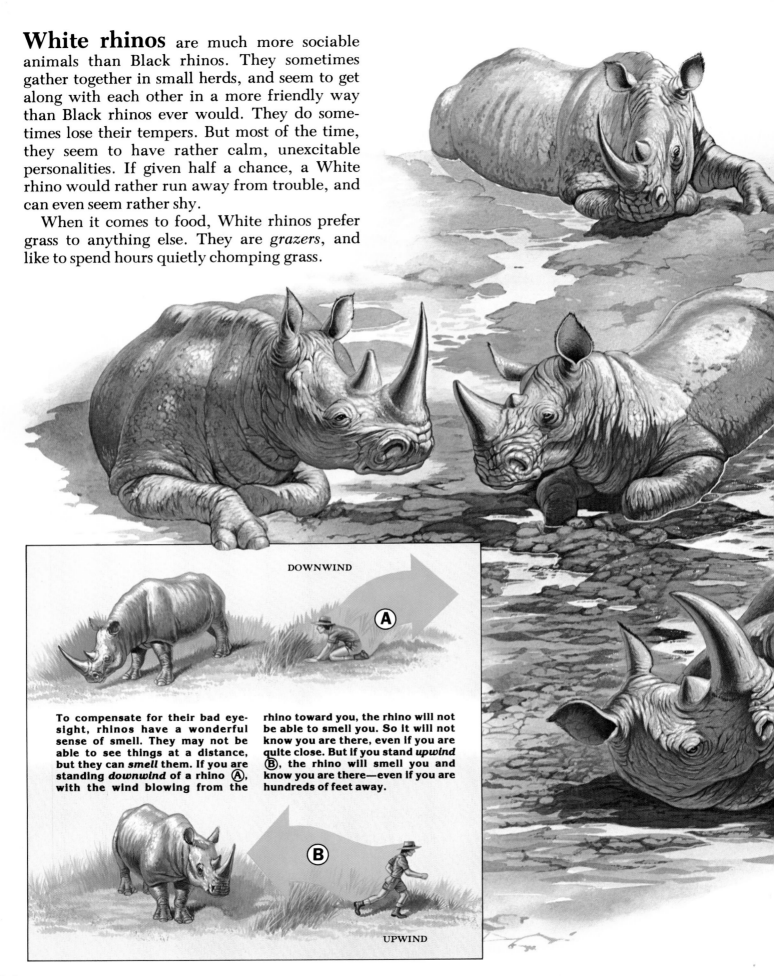

White rhinos are much more sociable animals than Black rhinos. They sometimes gather together in small herds, and seem to get along with each other in a more friendly way than Black rhinos ever would. They do sometimes lose their tempers. But most of the time, they seem to have rather calm, unexcitable personalities. If given half a chance, a White rhino would rather run away from trouble, and can even seem rather shy.

When it comes to food, White rhinos prefer grass to anything else. They are *grazers*, and like to spend hours quietly chomping grass.

DOWNWIND

(A)

To compensate for their bad eyesight, rhinos have a wonderful sense of smell. They may not be able to see things at a distance, but they can *smell* them. If you are standing *downwind* of a rhino Ⓐ, with the wind blowing from the rhino toward you, the rhino will not be able to smell you. So it will not know you are there, even if you are quite close. But if you stand *upwind* Ⓑ, the rhino will smell you and know you are there—even if you are hundreds of feet away.

(B)

UPWIND

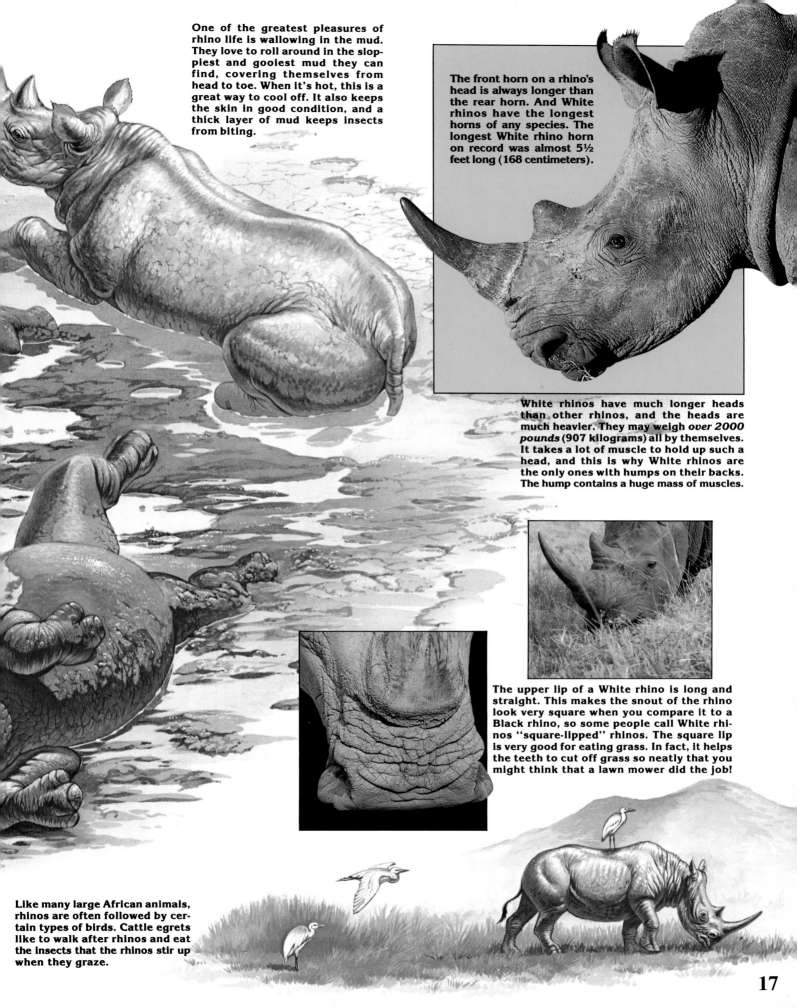

One of the greatest pleasures of rhino life is wallowing in the mud. They love to roll around in the sloppiest and gooiest mud they can find, covering themselves from head to toe. When it's hot, this is a great way to cool off. It also keeps the skin in good condition, and a thick layer of mud keeps insects from biting.

The front horn on a rhino's head is always longer than the rear horn. And White rhinos have the longest horns of any species. The longest White rhino horn on record was almost 5½ feet long (168 centimeters).

White rhinos have much longer heads than other rhinos, and the heads are much heavier. They may weigh *over 2000 pounds* (907 kilograms) all by themselves. It takes a lot of muscle to hold up such a head, and this is why White rhinos are the only ones with humps on their backs. The hump contains a huge mass of muscles.

The upper lip of a White rhino is long and straight. This makes the snout of the rhino look very square when you compare it to a Black rhino, so some people call White rhinos "square-lipped" rhinos. The square lip is very good for eating grass. In fact, it helps the teeth to cut off grass so neatly that you might think that a lawn mower did the job!

Like many large African animals, rhinos are often followed by certain types of birds. Cattle egrets like to walk after rhinos and eat the insects that the rhinos stir up when they graze.

17

Asian rhinos are quite different from the Black and White rhinos of Africa, and scientists believe that the two groups are only distantly related to each other. There are three types of Asian rhinos—the Great Indian rhino, the Javan rhino, and the Sumatran rhino.

Indian and Javan rhinos have only one horn, and they have the bumpy armored skin that most people think of when they think of rhinos. This makes Indian and Javan rhinos look quite different from the smoother-skinned African rhinos. The Sumatran rhino has two horns like African rhinos, but the horns are very small.

All of the Asian rhinos are browsers. But they live in different kinds of places, as you will see below—and this means that they eat different kinds of plants.

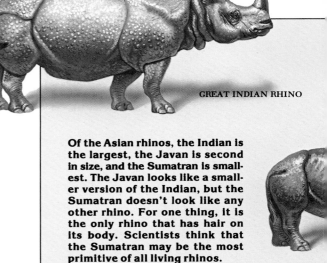
GREAT INDIAN RHINO

Of the Asian rhinos, the Indian is the largest, the Javan is second in size, and the Sumatran is smallest. The Javan looks like a smaller version of the Indian, but the Sumatran doesn't look like any other rhino. For one thing, it is the only rhino that has hair on its body. Scientists think that the Sumatran may be the most primitive of all living rhinos.

SUMATRAN RHINO

JAVAN RHINO

Unlike the rhinos of Africa, the rhinos of Asia do not live on open plains. Javan and Sumatran rhinos live in wooded areas, and spend most of their time in such dense forests that they are seldom seen. As you might expect, they are leaf-eaters.

Some people believe that the myth of the unicorn began with the one-horned rhinos of Asia. Hundreds of years ago, people in Europe didn't know what a rhino looked like. So, when they heard stories from travelers about an animal in Asia that had only one horn, they may have assumed that the animal looked like a horse. When they put a horse and one horn together, they invented the unicorn.

Indian rhinos prefer swampy areas, where there is a lot of water to drink and a lot of lush vegetation to eat.

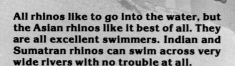

All rhinos like to go into the water, but the Asian rhinos like it best of all. They are all excellent swimmers. Indian and Sumatran rhinos can swim across very wide rivers with no trouble at all.

18

When rhino mothers defend their babies, they can be very fierce. In Asia, tigers sometimes try to catch baby rhinos. But they seldom get the chance to eat one, because their mothers put up such a good fight. In addition to her huge horn, an Indian rhino mother has large, sharp teeth that can easily cut through a tiger's skin.

JAVAN RHINO

Newborn rhinos are not helpless like human babies. Within an hour after they are born, they are up on their feet and trotting around after their mothers. Indian rhinos have the biggest babies. They may be two feet tall at birth (61 centimeters) and weigh between 80 and 125 pounds (36 and 57 kilograms).

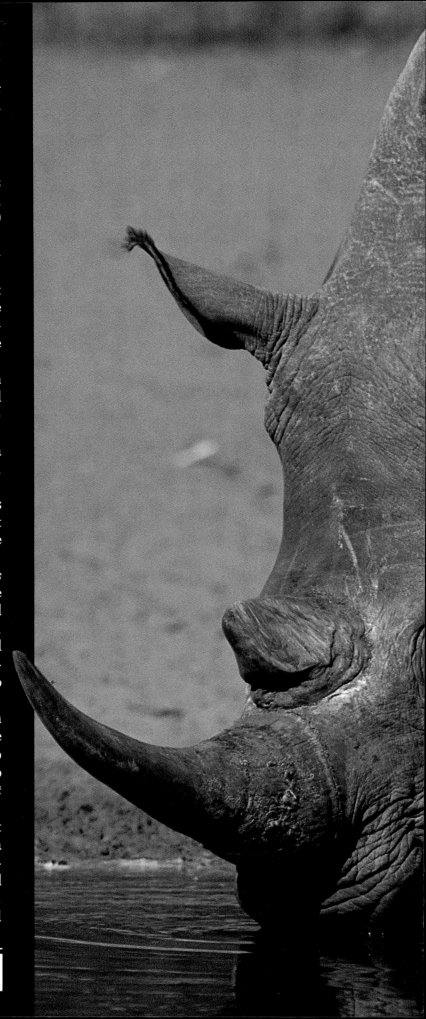

The future of rhinos in Africa and Asia looks bad. For the past 20 years, rhinos everywhere have been experiencing what biologists call a population "crash." The number of rhinos in all species has been going down faster and faster.

Today, rhinos are completely gone from hundreds of areas in which they were once found. And the remaining populations of some species have grown very small. There are fewer than 500 Sumatran rhinos left, and fewer than 60 Javan rhinos. It is hard to get exact information, but it looks as though the White rhinos of northern Africa may already be extinct.

There are several reasons for this. Like most other wild animals, rhinos are suffering because their habitat is being destroyed by people. Rhinos are found in parts of the world where the human population is growing most rapidly. And the human need for more food and land in these areas is so great that more and more land is taken away from rhinos (and other wildlife) every year.

But the worst threat to rhinos comes from a small group of people who kill rhinos illegally, so they can cut off their horns and sell them. Every place that rhinos live, there are laws against rhino hunting. But there is a huge profit to be made from rhino horns, so some evil people are willing to break the laws.

Rhino horn is extremely valuable — *twice as valuable as gold* in some places. Because some people think that it has wonderful medical and magical powers. In certain parts of the world, people believe that medicine made of powdered rhino horn will cure even the most serious diseases. And for this reason, they are willing to pay almost *any* price to get it.

Scientific tests have proved that rhino horn has no medical power at all — but the rhinos are still being killed. If a way can be found to stop this terrible business, it may not be too late to save the rhinos. But something must be done *at once*.

There are some encouraging signs that at least some rhinos will be saved. In South Africa, a program has been started to protect White rhinos from hunters and help them to breed. And the number of rhinos has increased as a result. In India, a similar program has led to a small increase in the number of Indian rhinos.

Index